Nana is Dying

Informing your child that a loved one is dying
Speaking to your child about death
Working through Grief

Facing the Difficulties of Life Series --#2

©June 18 2014

James Olah

Nana is Dying

Informing your child that a loved one is dying
Speaking to your child about death
Working through Grief

Facing the Difficulties of Life Series --#2

James Olah

©June 18, 2014
51 Pages, 16,000 words
Paper: ISBN-13:978-1500783433
Paper: ISBN-10:1500783439

HALO BOOKS

TABLE OF CONTENTS

INTRODUCTION – WHY THIS BOOK IS IMPORTANT

After writing most of this book's content I had a bright idea. On Facebook I requested friends to answer questions about how they either handled a situation with their children when talking about death or how their parents handled this difficult situation with them. I was looking for people's experiences to give me further insight into the needs I am addressing in this book. Was the direction of my book what people needed? Their answers affirm that I addressed the very issues they faced. I will share their accounts at the beginning of various chapters. The relevance of these stories reveals situations with which many will be able to identify.

One of the responses from my request came from a woman named Bonnie. She tells her account of how she was treated during the time her mother was dying and then of her mom's subsequent death. Bonnie was eight when this happened. Along with all the contributors she gave me permission to quote her response. As you read Bonnie's account you will understand why I chose her story to begin my book.

> *I'm responding as an individual that lost her mother at the age of 8. The easiest way for me to answer your questions is to give you a clear picture of how it was for me from the eyes of an 8 year old.*

> *I remember going to school Jan 18, 1990 with my mom walking me to the elementary school. When school ended my mom was not there to pick me up as usual. Instead, all of a sudden I was going to stay with my father. I only saw him every other weekend (if he would show up) so, I thought it was a special treat. I remember a lot of quiet talk by adult family members when I was around them. I remember bouncing between my father, his girl friend, and my paternal grandparents for quite a bit. I remember*

missing my mom and wanting to go home but, I couldn't understand why I couldn't. I didn't get straight answers from anyone. I discovered later that that my mom was actually in a coma, and the adults thought that my older sister and I were too young to see her during her hospital stay.

On March 3, 1990 my older sister and I were at my soon to be step-ma's house. My father and step mom were present. I recall the phone ringing, and my father going to the back of the modular home to talk. He called my sister in the back room, and she took the phone call.

At that time all I remember is my sister coming into the living room, bawling her eyes out, my step mom and dad were crying and trying to comfort us. I started to cry because everyone else was crying. I didn't learn of my mom's death until I was at the funeral home for the showing. I didn't understand death. I didn't even recognize my mom in the casket. This was my first experience of the death of someone I knew. That day was a complete blur to me. I don't recall the questions I asked, or what family said to provide comfort. What I do remember is that for a very long time I blamed myself for my mom being gone. I thought it was my fault. I thought "maybe if I was better and a good girl, she would come back". I remember wanting to go be with her in heaven. I would ask in my prayers to go to heaven too. I would ask to die.

It was such a trying time for me. I needed the mother and daughter bonding experience. I went through a lot of therapy to get me through all my confusion and childhood pains.

I think it would have been helpful for someone to have spoken to me about things in advance. I needed to hear that my mom was sick. I also needed to know that it wasn't looking good for her. I needed a simple explanation of heaven. I needed to know that when someone can't be with us here anymore that is where they go. Every child is different; some understand things at younger ages more so than others. Although, I was raised in a religious life style, I still did not comprehend heaven, hell, God, good and bad, etc.

5

Following my mom's death I sought out affection from everyone around me. I would sit on my aunt's lap; I wanted to be around adults more than kids. I wanted to be snuggled and told that I was loved. Now that I look back I think that I really annoyed some adults.

I have had many conversations with others regarding this. I think it would have been better for me personally to see my mom while she was still ill. I understand that I was being protected but, as a child - it would have been nice to be able to say "I love you" one more time. (Bonnie)

Have you had a similar experience? Have you been in a situation where you didn't know what to say to your young children about Nana's death? Perhaps you wondered what you should tell them. If you had a bad experience in the way you were treated by your parents when you were a child, then this task of telling your child may be much harder for you. If you fear death and have no hope in an afterlife then talking about death may be very difficult for you to be open in talking with your children. My desire is that this book will offer the kind of advice that gives you light in a dark time of your life.

A short word about this book

We can talk about all kinds of scenarios that children face. A friend had a heart attack or was killed in an accident. Grandma or grandpa is dying. Dad was killed in war or a car accident. Mom has cancer. Uncle Ned died unexpectedly. The neighbor friend, Jason, died of a bee sting. There is a plethora of ways a person dies and various situations.

Instead of seeking to include every kind of scenario in this book, I will simplify it by just talking about grandma dying. We will call her Nana. The issue is not who is dying but how we help our children face the dying process, or the death of a loved one or friend. Finally we want to focus on what we can do to help them work through the grieving process.

CHAPTER ONE: MY EXPERIENCE

I was a pastor for 39 years and served as a Hospice Chaplain for about three years. One of the questions that came up over the years is *"how do I tell my child about the death of grandma or dad or a friend?"*

Early in my ministry talking to children about someone's death set me on edge. Just because I was a pastor didn't mean I knew exactly what to say, nor did that automatically make it easy to talk with the child about death and dying.

It is understandable that parents want to protect their children. They want their children to face the harsh realities of life without scarring them for the rest of their life. None of us like to see our children hurt. We look for ways to protect them from the major upsets of life as long as possible. For various reasons some parents mistakenly think that they need to protect their children from all the harsh realities of life. They mistakenly think that their protection will make life easier for their children. What is often overlooked is the truth that if we don't help them face tragedies honestly as a child then we can be setting them up for greater problems later on when they face their own trials. Children need to learn how to deal honesty with the difficulties of life. This is your opportunity to prepare them to face the hardships of life.

I don't come at this as an expert on this topic, but a fellow traveler through life, seeking to understand the needs of those we love and how we can best assist them. You don't have to be a professional to help your child face the difficult realities of life. That which will help you is good information that directs you in how to help them process some difficult information and then go on with life. Even though it seems hard for some to address the issues of dying and death, we need to make sure that we don't make things more complex than need be.

I call myself a fellow traveler on this road of life when it comes to dealing with grief. When I entered the ministry I was the typical man who really didn't express emotions well. I am not the type that just knows what to say when people are going thought difficult times. I admire those who can effortlessly express compassion and grace to people in the tragedies of life. My style is to be there, listen, and answer questions when appropriate. I admire people who easily offer comforting words from the heart at the right time. My tongue locks up and my mind goes into neutral in these situations. In my mind I feel like a wide eyed deer caught in the car headlights and won't move for what seems like the longest time. I'm sure many can identify with that.

I say all of this to let you know that, even if you feel like I do, you can learn how to deal with these emotionally difficult situations. I learned how to respond to people in such circumstances by reading, going to grief seminars and then just putting what I learned into practice. I did not shy away from such situations. The one thing that I didn't have to learn so much was the compassion and love I have for people. That is what helped me to learn and grow in my ability to deal with people in the hurting moments of life. Perhaps you readily identify with me in this last area. You have a genuine love for your child, and you desire the best for them, and want to help them face this very difficult situation in an honest manner. You are just looking for help in how to do it.

Death of My Wife:

Being with people who are dealing with death, injury and tragedy was a part of my ministry for more than forty years. I've been in the emergency room, I've been with families as their loved one was dying and helped them face their death, and I've officiated at a couple of hundred funerals. Through those experiences I've learned a lot.

It is one thing to walk with others through their times of loss, it is another to walk through it with your own loved one. It was just over six weeks after I retired that we discovered that my wife had cancer. Sixty seven days later she died. During that time I maintained open conversation with my two adult children, related emotionally with them, and communicated often with my grandchildren about the process of dying and how they were facing the loss. We talked openly and freely.

We provided the children with an friendly and candid atmosphere in which they were able to ask any question they wanted, and they got as complete an answer as we could give. Our knowledge was also limited as to what was happening at times. My youngest daughter felt that in the last days of my wife's life that the grandchildren should not see Nana. After my wife died the children (ages 5 and 9) were allowed to come to the funeral home and encouraged to touch Nana and say good bye. We answered their questions and took time to listen to what they had to say. We talked to them about the various expressions of grief and gave them freedom to express themselves. Most importantly we loved on them.

The grieving process didn't suddenly subside after the funeral. There continued to be lot of discussion, commiserating and tears about our loss. The initial grieving of the loss lasts several weeks. However the process of grieving is more like a series of waves that come and go during the first year and more so on various anniversary dates. For us it was the first Easter, Mother's day, her birthday, our anniversary, the kid's birthdays, Thanksgiving and Christmas. Each reminded us of the loss in a different way. As we got farther away from her death it reminded us of the permanence of her death.

There was a specific event that strained our aching hearts. This happened two months after my wife's death. My wife's absence from the family was felt with great intensity when my oldest daughter got married and mom wasn't there to be a part of the proceedings and celebrate this long awaited marriage.

Facing death with openness and honesty is important, but it doesn't release you from the harsh reality and pain of losing a loved one. Continuing to be open and honest in talking about the loss does allow you to cope and go on with confidence and greater peace. Not talking holds you in a type of bondage that keeps you in the grieving cycle.

Being open, honest, and compassionate with your children is the key to helping them navigate the troubled waters of the dying and death situations your family will face. These are important elements, not just when you have to tell them about Nana's death, but it is also foundational in helping them work through their grieving process. Your openness, with which you begin this journey, will set the tone for the rest of the process.

That which may make your grief more difficult, in helping your children, is that you too are going through a great loss in your life. You may not always have the emotional energy, the patience or the words to help your children during the weeks and months that follow their death. That is why it is good to have a parent, friend or pastor who can help address issues with your children when those times get too tough for you. Don't be afraid to ask for help. In fact, make it a point to ask for help.

Two years after my wife died I still talk with my grandchildren about Nana. They are now seven and eleven. Recently I was with my grandson and he asked me about Nana, and we just talked about some of the fun things we did and what she was like. Children start to forget and they need to be reminded. There are times we have cried together because we miss her so much. It's good for children to see parents cry over a loss. That allows them freedom to express their emotions in an appropriate manner. Don't seek to humiliate your children into avoiding the emotions of grief by saying such things as 'suck it up', or 'be a man' or 'real men don't cry'. It doesn't solve their problem, or help them really deal with difficulties.

There's one last thing about my story that I would like to share. I mentioned that the children tend to forget about the person who dies. Before my wife died we discussed something we wanted to do for our children. We talked about each of our children and what they meant to us and how they had made us proud. Nancy then asked me to write a letter to each of the children expressing these things to them.

Over the next few months, after my wife died, I wrote separate letters addressing different topics. These letters were to both of our daughters, to their husbands and to our two grandchildren. We wanted them to have something personal by which they could remember specifics, and know how much we loved them and how they made us proud. To the two grandchildren I not only expressed our love but took the time to give them history of Nana and me so they could reflect and remember specific details about us. Then this year I put together a photo album of pictures with me and my wife and that child in it. It was designed so they could remember specifics of things we did together as well as special events. The grieving process is not to make us forget but to help us appreciate the part they had in our life and heart.

CHAPTER TWO: BE HONEST ABOUT DEATH

Death is clouded with fantasy:

I am part of a group that is involved with nationals in Burma (Myanmar). We were working with them on translating a Bible and I was heading up the computer team state side. We needed to talk face to face with the translators and get some translation methods straightened out; thus started my adventure of traveling to a third world country. As I prepared for the trip I received all kinds of advice. Some was good and some not very accurate. I didn't know what it would be like to be in a third world culture. What to eat and not eat was a big concern. The horror stories I heard created a lot of misconceptions in my mind. I sought to learn from people who traveled in that area of the world. But after the time I spent there I gained more of an accurate perception of what it is like to visit a third world country. My inexperience caused me to contemplate all kinds of fears, both real and imagined. Talking with people who had regular experiences with foreign travel and having someone very experienced going with me on the trip sure helped out a lot.

Just as I needed someone experienced to help me through my trip, so your children need someone who has experience to help them on their journey through the dying and death experience of a loved one. Think about this. *Do you understand death completely?* None of us fully understands death on this side of the grave. If we have a limited understanding, then it certainly stands to reason that our children know much less than we do about death.

Children today are often isolated from death and dying and the tragedies of life. In former eras children saw people get sick, even helped their parents in caring for these sick people and then that person died in their own home. The wake was in their home as well. Children were part of the procession of going to the cemetery and burying their loved ones.

Maybe an older child helped dad or mom dig the grave. Mortality was higher and maybe they saw brothers and sisters die. Wars were not kept to battle fields, but were in their villages and walled cities. Death was a part of life that they learned to take for granted. They had a realistic view of death.

Think about what modern children see. They have been taught by the entertainment industry that sanitizes and minimizes death. They see cartoon characters get killed off and then come back to life. They see people killed and there is seldom any emotion about the death of a person unless that is the focus of the movie. The good guy never dies and neither do the beautiful women. Mostly the bad people are killed off.

In the animated movie "Tangled" we see at the end of the movie that Flynn, Rapunzel's new love, is stabbed by Gothel. In his dying act he sets Rapunzel free by cutting her hair off. As she cries over him, she sings and her tears drop on his face and he is brought back to life. That is a scene touched with emotion to your child. But what does your child see in this act? They think that people can be brought back to life if there is enough love. Show children fantasy enough and they think it is true. It is fantasy to think that special individuals have the power to bring dead people back to life. This kind of fantasy is what children are learning, and so when a loved one dies they may strongly expect someone to come along and bring Nana back to life. They may also think that she is not really gone forever.

Your older children like different movies. In the Harry Potter movie "Half Blood Prince" the book ends with Snape casting the killing spell Avada Kedavra on Dumbledore. This is Harry's mentor whom he loved dearly. Certainly he would not stay dead. Dumbledore was a powerful wizard! At the memorial service there are all the wizards and witches who have these great powers and it is so easy to think that someone might do something to bring Dumbledore back to life. Even though he is not brought back to life Dumbledore does appear to Harry to advise him and help him bring down Lord Voldemort. Harry Potter is fiction and it makes for good story with Dumbledore helping him, but it is not reality. If children don't have a hold on the reality of death then such false thinking sticks in the back of children's minds as to the reality of Nana's death.

Have you talked with your children about their thoughts of death? Do they recognize the permanence of death? Do they think that Nana will communicate with them and guide them in the difficult times of life? If so they will feel disappointment and heart broken when that does not happen and reality sets in.

More than ever our children have been influenced by the make-believe aspect of movies and books. It is important for us to deal with our children in an honest and forthright manner. If you are reading this book and nothing tragic has taken place yet, plan on talking about the reality and facts of death with your children. A parent's responsibility is to prepare children to face the real world and all that life throws at them. Teach them about death. Don't get mysterious with them, just talk in a matter-of-fact kind of way. Avoid passing your fear of death onto them.

Here are some thoughts that can provide good conversation starters. Have you thought about death? What do you think it is? What happens to a person when they die? What concerns do you have when you think about death? Those who are people of faith should relate your faith to death. When they share their answers listen to all they have to say without correcting them. Ask meaningful questions to help them go deeper.

What your child needs to know about Death:

In the article: *Children and Grief: What They Know, How They Feel, How to Help,* Robin F. Goodman, Ph.D.[1] makes some good basic statements that guide us into areas that children need to know when talking about dying and death.

Dr. Goodman says children need to know the following truths about death:

1. Death is irreversible
2. All life functions end completely at the time of death.
3. Everything that is alive eventually dies.
4. There are physical reasons why someone dies.

We know these truths for they are so basic to our understanding. These are good talking points when communicating with your children about death. Children should start learning such truths as young as preschool. You can take incidents that happen on television and use it as a teaching tool. Talking to your children about death is not a lecture, but a talking subject. Don't tell them each of the above points at once, but look for your teaching moments to introduce or reinforce the concept of these truths.

When talking with your child about death be sure to share some of your discovery points about death as you matured. What were some of your misconceptions? What did it feel like when you came to understand some of the realities of death? What fears did you experience? How did you deal with death of the first person you knew personally? What were some of your concerns? What helped you? The more personal you make your explanations the more they can identify with the truths you share.

Death is irreversible:

The first time a child goes into a funeral home and looks at the person in the casket they think the person is just asleep and will soon awaken. Children don't comprehend the reality of the permanence of death. It doesn't sink in, and so it is easy to think that the person will certainly get up. Maybe death is like a long vacation and they will see them come back into their life again. That's how uninformed children can think. They need to know that when a person dies nothing about their state of being is going to change on earth. This condition is permanent. When I was young, I went to the funeral home to see my grandfather, the mystery of death caused me to also think that he was sleeping and could get up at any time. After years of experience this thought does not even cross my mind any more. Experience helps us see the reality of death, and most children have not yet had any experience with being around a dead person.

All life functions end completely at the time of death:

Another needful truth your child should understand is that when a person dies they get cold. If there is a viewing of the body at the funeral home, allow your child to touch Nana for this helps them experience one of the realities of death. Make sure you tell them what to expect. This is also a good time to tell them that the coldness they feel is an indication that the body isn't working any more. I think the coldness of the body hit me so hard when I kissed my wife good bye. All the warmth of her living body was gone.

Everything that is alive will eventually die:

We have the reality that people don't come back to life, but children have to learn it. It is not wrong for your child to know that we will all die one day. The Bible reminds us *"It is appointed onto man once to die…"[2]* No one escapes death. Should you or can you really promise your children that you will ALWAYS be there for them? Can anyone really promise that? As long as you are alive you can be there for them. If you shield them from the truth that you could die and you do, then that means that you didn't keep your word to them. None of us has full control over how long we will live, neither do we choose when we will die. Don't beat your child over the head with this truth, but this is general information they need to know. Don't scare them with this teaching, but talk about it in a matter-of-fact kind of way so they understand death's reality. Don't allow your personal fear to scare them.

When a pet dies they want to know what happened to it. Why is it not moving anymore? Why can't I play with it? When the child asks these questions, realize they may also want to know if that could happen to them. This becomes even more of a concern when a loved one dies or a friend who is closer to their age. Children are curious about death and want to know honest details about it.

There are physical reasons someone dies:

They need to know why Grandma died. It was discovered that my wife was in stage four of renal cancer. That means that it had already spread to various parts of her body. We told our grandchildren what it was and how it affected different parts of her body. If you don't tell them why Grandma died then they will come up with their own uninformed, reasons.

Inform them that people die for a lot of reasons. Sometimes people get a disease like cancer or heart disease and they die. Sometimes people are killed in accidents or in war. Sometimes evil people kill others. Tell them that your job is to watch over them and make sure things like that don't happen. That is why you tell them to be careful around busy streets, and not go with strangers or play in dangerous areas. You don't want something to happen to them, and you don't want them to die.

All of this is easier if you start talking about death before anyone they know is dying or has died. Your job, as a parent, is to help them face the realities of life in an honest and informed way.

CHAPTER THREE: TELLING YOUR CHILD THAT NANA IS DYING OR HAS DIED?

Lessons from Tee Ball:

One of my granddaughters was playing on a Tee Ball team this year. It was most humorous watching children, who know nothing about baseball, play for the first time. They didn't know the rules of the game. Some would come up to the tee and stand behind the ball to hit it. The first time some of the kids hit the ball they ran after the ball to get it. In that first game they hit the ball and were told to run to first base. Some ran after the ball. Some ran to second base via the pitcher's mound. Some ran to third base. Some just stood there not knowing what to do.

We smile at what they do and think how little they know about the game. As the season progressed I noticed that they were starting to understand the basic principles of the game. They came up to the plate and hit properly. They ran to the correct base each time. They learned that they needed to run to the next base when the next person hit the ball. The fielders learned where to throw the ball. Repetitively doing something, and watching others do it right, and listening to the adults, helped them learn the fundamentals of playing baseball.

There is a sense in which each of us is like those five and six years olds playing Tee Ball. It is when life demands that we tell our children about very difficult situations of life, and helping them through the grieving process after Nana dies. We don't know the rules of what we should do. We feel clumsy and trip over our words or say the wrong things. We get frustrated because we don't know what to say or how to help. Our fear may cause us to clam up and tell them nothing. We feel as frustrated and confused as the Tee Ball players.

I used the Tee Ball illustration to help you realize the reason you may have a problem is because you just haven't had experience running the bases of grief. Just as the Tee Ball coach instructs the children what to do, so all you need is a coach to give you the correct information to help you guide your children through their difficult time. If you keep working at it then the process will become more familiar and you will gain your confidence.

Guidelines for the Game:

Personal experiences of parents better equip them to tell their children of terminal sickness, death or difficult situations that can help their child cope. You can gain from their experiences and in turn offer practical guidelines to help your child maneuver through the troubled waters that come upon your family.

Situations vary about Nana's death. She can die of a disease or she can die suddenly from a heart attack or stroke. If she dies of a disease it can be a long or short process. Children need to have time with Nana, even as she is declining. When you tell your child about her disease or death here are some guidelines experienced people offer for your benefit.

A. *Tell the truth.* Well-meaning adults may try to distract children by telling half-truths. Some think it is acceptable to lie to children about the death of someone they love. Parents, seeking to protect themselves from having to address the full impact of a child's grief, skirt the issue of speaking the truth by thinking that children are "too young" to know what is going on. Lisa Athan[3] from Grief Speak, in her article: Talking to Children about Death says: "*When families join together to face a crisis and the adults are willing and open to talk to the children and answer their questions, the crisis becomes more manageable.*"

Don't beat around the bush. Be direct and use appropriate language for their age when you inform them that Nana is in the hospital and we don't know how much longer she is going to live. If Nana died then say something simple like: "*I need to tell you that Nana died last night while you were sleeping.*" You may think that not telling the truth will shelter them from the harshness of

18

death. If you don't tell the truth that Grandma is dying then when Grandma dies they will learn the truth. Informing your child of the truth gives them a longer time to process the information. It also gives you opportunity to talk about some of the issues of death.

Telling them the truth does not mean that you have to tell them all the details. That depends on their age and their ability to comprehend. Truth is very important for them in dealing with difficult situations. Answer all their questions as honestly and completely as you can. Their questions will give you guide lines as to how much you need to tell them. Don't be afraid to tell them you don't know all the answers at this time.

B. *Use the term "death" when referring to what happened.* Don't seek to make the experience more palatable by avoiding the term death when talking about Nana. By using some other term death doesn't seem as final. When I conduct a funeral service I use the term death when speaking about the deceased to ingrain in my audience the reality of the condition of the person.

Sometimes the adult's fear of death prevents them from speaking to the children openly. If you said Nana has fallen asleep then the child thinks she will awake. Or maybe the child won't want to "fall asleep" because death happens when I fall asleep. They may fear they may never get up. Another avoidance technique is telling the child that Nana went on a long, long trip and won't be coming back. But the child thinks that people always come back from trips. Maybe the child won't want to take trips with you because they want to come back home. Don't be afraid to use the terms dying, die, or death with your child when talking about a person who is dying or has died. Help them live in reality.

The way you talk about something doesn't change what happened. But the honest way you talk about death affects how your child will view death later on.

C. *Truth should be simple and direct.* We like to sugar coat bad news, but as we think of how to break the news we need to make sure we don't become evasive of the truth. Telling your child about the condition of Nana can be as simple as this: *"Nana is very sick, and*

19

it looks like she is not going to get better, she may die soon." Allow them to ask questions about what is wrong with Nana. If you know that Nana is going to die soon, then tell them simply and straightforward: *"The doctors told us that Nana will not live very much longer."*

D. *Allow children to ask questions.* Children are not comforted by being kept in the dark. Just like you want to be brought into the light in a situation, so do your children. Answer their questions honestly. When you don't know the facts, don't make up an answer, but inform them that you don't know all the answers.

I used to have a special time in our church services called "Ask the Pastor" and they could ask me any question. I would tell them I have an answer to every question. It might be *"I don't know"*. What I'm saying is that none of us has all the answers to life. This is unexplored territory to your child so they want to know how to process this new information about someone they love dearly. Ignorance keeps them in bondage. You can help loose them from that bondage by speaking the truth. Be open and honest and answer the question to the best of your ability. If you don't know the answer, tell them that you will seek to get an answer, if it is possible. It is also honest, if it is true, to tell them that there are some questions we can't answer in this life.

E. *Be sensitive to their emotional responses.* Your child may not know how to grieve and the thought of the loss of someone dear to them may be more than they can bear. Hold them, be gentle and kind to them and encourage them. Much compassion is needed during this time. After they have settled down tell them that the reason they have so much emotion is because they have so much love for Nana and it hurts inside to lose her. Shying away from their own emotion doesn't help them. Don't let their emotions scare you. Emotions are natural responses to our losses in life. Encourage them to express emotions.
- Don't scold them for being loud or going out of control.
- Don't minimize their emotional responses.
- Don't deny boys the opportunity to cry.
- Don't tell them to *buck up* because of your fear of emotion.

F. *Provide opportunities for them to express their emotions.* After my wife died I expressed my grief through talking about my wife, and telling her story, and listening to music about heaven. I would sit and listen, and cry as I heard the songs that touched my heart.

Children express their grief in much the same way as an adult. They may also express their emotions in different ways. Adults tend to talk and maybe cry. Children will do that too. Children are also comfortable expressing their grief through drawing, singing or writing. Provide photos that focus on Nana and something that they used to do together. This helps them express their love for her in specific ways.

Children need the freedom to talk out their feelings. Some will feel comfortable journaling. They are learning to do this more in school these days. Give them a notebook and encourage them to write about Nana and the way they remember her, and the things they enjoyed doing with her. Give them ideas of what to write about. "Why not write about the vacation you took with Nana and Papa last summer? Another time tell them to write about the week they spent with Nana and Papa during winter break. What did you enjoy most about your time with them?"

G. *Allow your child personal time.* The separation and loss caused by death is traumatic to them. Allow them to have time to process what happened and the new emotions they are experiencing. They have no idea what this is going to be like in the future without Nana and need time to think about it. However, you want to make sure there is not excessive time alone. If they shut themselves in their room every day, then they need your help because they are not coping properly.

H. *Don't just talk, use your ears.* If you are a nervous, or a non-stop talker it is easy to dominate the conversation. You may know what they are going through, but they need to express it themselves. Doing all the talking and thinking for your child is not good for them. Make sure you give them your undivided attention and listen to what they have to say. Take what they say seriously. Clarify what they are telling you, so you get an accurate picture of what they are saying. Ask questions about what they said. Have them explain things to you. Remember, you are not interrogating them. Be open with them when they want to talk. Look for ways to draw them out by asking questions that are appropriate to what they are talking about. Sit with them. Get at eye level.

My daughter and granddaughter would sit on a couch and cuddle as they talked and oft times cried when thinking about Nana. Children need the closeness of physical contact. Physical touch means a lot to your children, especially in their time of grief, *for it gives them needed connection in a time when they feel loss.* Even if you are not comfortable with being physical, do it for them. Physically connecting in difficult times builds bonds in your relationship that can be strengthened in no other way.

I. *Find a support group.* Don't feel like you have to go through this grief alone with your child. Have other people talk with your child. There is the school counselor, a sensitive relative, a pastor or children's worker at church. If you find you can't handle the situation with your child, because they are going deep into depression, don't hesitate to go to a grief counselor. Make sure you get help if you are having a hard time coping. Many churches, funeral homes, and hospices offer free grief support groups. Many hospices allow those who they have not serviced to be included in their grief support groups.

You need to be healthy to have healthy conversations with your child, so get help if you need it. It was about two years after my wife's death before my daughter attended a grief class. She said she wished she had attended sooner after mom died, for the grief class would have been more helpful during the intense part of the grieving process instead of almost two years later.

J. *Don't project your fears on the child.* There is nothing wrong with having emotions, even when you tell your children about your loved one's death. Be careful to not project your fears on them. What does that mean? Projecting fear is transferring your fear and strengthening their own fears every time you talk to them. A person who doesn't have fear is not always asking them if they are afraid of something. Those who keep talking about a specific fear make the child more aware of something that at first was no big issue, but the more you focus on the fear the greater it becomes to them. Children can very easily pick up moods and feelings from their parents. What are you projecting that your children notice? Is it fear or confidence? Is it healthy or destructive? Is there an issue you need to address in your own life? Resources to help your are abundant. If you don't want to see a counselor then you might want to find some internet articles that address your issue or find a good book that can help you work through your fears or issues.

K. *After you explain something get feedback from them.* When you explain a new concept to children find out how they comprehended what you said. Following your explanation, ask them to put it in their own words what they heard you say. They may not have heard all the detail because they are distracted by other things cluttering their mind. This kind of questioning helps you to know if you are getting your message across to them and what needs to be clarified. After all, when you are learning something new, not every fact sticks to the walls of your mind during the first explanation. Bear in mind that you are taking your child from the unknown into the known, from darkness into light. It can be a slow process, so be patient and kind with your child. You may have to explain something several times before they comprehend. Avoid belittling or laughing at their perception of what you said.

L. *Importance of touch.* Touch is so important during this time of grief. When you inform them of someone dying or who has died, make sure you give them hugs. Hugging is their connection in a time when death makes them feel disconnected. It is something from which we all draw strength. Notice people when you go into a funeral home. Those who are distraught, as they come in, are comforted by a hug or a warm handshake. In this time of need we draw strength from those we love by this physical contact. Your children may need you to hug them or cuddle up in a chair with them. Recollect what Bonnie said in the introduction about the need of being with adults, and sitting on their laps, and being hugged and having love affirmed.

Not everyone grieves the same way. That will be recognized in Amy's story in the next chapter. Be sensitive to the needs of your child and the way they are responding to Nana's death. Don't push ideas or questions on them that they don't seem to be interested in, or are not ready to discuss. Talk freely with them. I have been in some small group studies and noticed that the more transparent the leaders are the more readily the class opens up about their own lives. Transparency is just talking freely about the death of Nana and your feelings and memories. Doing this is something that will give your child freedom to open up as well.

CHAPTER FOUR: GOOD GRIEF - EMOTIONS.

Amy's Story:

Here is Amy's account that she related about the process of talking to her sons about her father's extended illness. You will hear some of her fears and frustrations. These are her responses to my questions. I have added personal comments in parentheses.

Q. As you look back on the death you faced, what kind of information would have helped you in informing your child that a loved one was dying?

A. We knew my dad was not in good health, and we never knew how much time we had left with him, but would not have considered him "dying." It was hard for me to prepare the boys for the possibility that he could die without making them afraid that he would die. I suppose that would have been the most helpful thing for me, just knowing how to balance that.

Q. What kind of frustration did you experience of knowing what to tell your child?

A. Every time my dad would go into the hospital, I felt like I wanted to reassure them, but I couldn't tell them everything would be okay because I didn't know that for sure. I didn't want to set them up for disappointment. How do you help a child understand that God's plan is always good, even when life hurts? And when you yourself are struggling to understand why God allows certain things that makes it even harder.

(Amy is a strong woman of faith, but that doesn't mean that she always knows what to say or how to relate God to each aspect of the difficult situation. She had to deal with her own struggles. Walking by faith means we trust God even though we don't know God's timeline or what He is seeking to accomplish.)

Q. Did you know how much information was enough or too much?

A. *Not always, but my dad gave my boys a precious gift before he died. He sat them down and told them that, eventually, something would happen and he wouldn't pull through. He told them it was okay to be sad, but that they should remember he was in heaven with Jesus, and he wasn't sick or suffering anymore, because in heaven he would be healthy and have both legs. I didn't know he had that conversation with them until after he was gone, and my son told me about it. He said it was really helpful for him in dealing with my dad's death*

(When a person is not afraid of death it is really helpful to talk with grandchildren or children about your death. Death may be a long way in the future but you can talk about your hope and confidence. Even if you are at the start of declining health, share your faith and hope with your family. Let them hear your words of confidence about being right with God. This will help them to eventually better deal with your death.)

Q. What concerned you most about how much information about the impending death your child could handle?

A. *Our situation was a little different, because we didn't know he was going to die, we just knew his life was fragile. I didn't want them living in fear all the time or be afraid that every time we said goodbye might be the last. I just wanted them to enjoy their time with him.*

(We have to discern how much information children are able to carry. What might be interesting is to talk with her children five years after his death and ask how much information they thought they may have been able to handle.)

Q. What do you feel were the right things you said to your children?

A. *Well, because my boys were older, we could have had more in-depth conversations about God's plan for us. I was honest with them about the fact that God's plan for my dad might be to take him to heaven, and that, although it would be hard for us, it was the best thing that could happen to him. We talked about heaven and how wonderful it is, and that Grandpa just got to go there sooner than we do.*

Q. What kind of things did you find helpful or frustrating as you helped your child through the grieving process?

A. *My boys grieved very differently. One son was not able to make the hurt stop. Sometimes all I could do was sit there and cry right along with him. We had some hard nights. I wanted him to know it was okay to cry and be sad. The other son didn't really cry or show a lot of emotion. That's just the way he is. That was frustrating for me in itself, because I didn't know how he was feeling. He didn't want to be smothered or held, just allowed to process things on his own. At first I was concerned that he was denying his grief, but now I know he wasn't, he just needed to work through it alone. I think knowing their different personalities was helpful in knowing how to comfort them.*

(This was an important discovery Amy made. People grieve differently. Men usually grieve differently than women. If you are interested in furthering your understanding in this area, do an internet search on how men grieve. Here are a couple of links to get you started: http://www.griefspeaks.com/id38.html http://thegrieftoolbox.com/article/what-women-should-know-about-male-grief Also Google how children grieve.)

Emotions of Grief:

When it comes to talking to your children about a terminal illness or the death of a loved one, does that cause your heart to race, do you get nervous, or perhaps tighten up inside? Does it concern you how your child will react? Your reaction will be based on various reasons. It may be because you had a bad childhood experience. You may not know what to say or how to say it. You may not know how much information to give your child. You are concerned about your child's reaction. Becoming equipped is more than knowing what to say, but also to recognize various kinds of reactions your child may express.

A grieving child may surprise you. Even though your child was so well behaved before Nana's death, you may find that he or she may be acting out, and not as compliant as before. After all, there is a fountain of emotion that has been unleashed, and that may be a new experience they've never had before and they don't know how to handle it.

The more you understand about the typical kinds of responses children have, the more patient you can be with them in handling them in this difficult time. If you think that only sadness and crying are typical in grief, then you won't be ready for other responses. Their emotional responses are coming at a time when you may not have a lot of extra emotional energy. To be aware of these emotional expressions will equip you to better handle them in a sensitive manner.

Notice all the typical emotions you observe at a funeral home. Some will be crying, some will be talking fondly about the person and the good memories, some will talk about how the person influenced their life, and some will be laughing and joking about their memories of the deceased. These are all appropriate emotions at a funeral. Children will also have various kinds of emotions in working through Nana's death. Understanding the various expressions of emotion will assist you in helping them cope during this time.

A.   *Sadness.* This can be expressed through facial sadness, withdrawal and going quiet or shedding tears. Make sure you let the school and their teacher know of the loss in your child's life. Children don't know when they will be overtaken by their grief and start crying. It helps to have understanding adults there who can facilitate their emotions during this time.

B.   *Anger.* Anger is also an emotion with which your child may have to deal. Most anger is usually based in fear. Your child will have fear of how they are going to cope. What will happen in their home? Who can they go to when they need help or just to talk?

Anger can be expressed against God. God is all powerful, why didn't He help Nana? Did He not love her? Is He punishing us or her?

They may feel that life is not fair or that it is unjust. Why did the drunk come out of the accident without a scratch and my loved one got killed? Sometimes they can be angry at the person who died. That person said they would always be there for me and now they have left.

It is important that your child finds proper expression of their anger, for if left unexpressed, anger can turn into depression, or it can go out of control and cause them to act out. In today's society we see a lot of angry young people. Why? It is because parents have mistreated them or in many cases abandoned them. Think about it, every single-parent home experiences the abandonment of one parent and that affects children. Help them find a positive expression of that energy. Physical exercise can help a lot during this time. They also need the friendship of their parent and other trusted adults. They need some form of expression of their inner feelings.

C. *Abandoned*. Feeling abandoned by their loved one is a reality on which they may be focusing their attention. They now have to go life alone. Why did grandma leave me? If you are divorced and aren't always with your children when they experience a death, make sure you spend extra time with them. They need to know you have not abandoned them because such feelings become more intense in the wake of a loss.

D. *Confusion*. During such emotional trauma people don't always think clearly. You may have to repeat things to your child. They may be going through the motions without realizing what they are doing. They may have glazed eyes because they can't concentrate on anything. Be patient and gracious in repeating instruction to them.

E. *Irritable*. They might become easily annoyed or exasperated. With the intense emotions they may have a hard time responding properly. They can snap at you for no apparent reason. This is one of the less explosive expressions of their anger.

F.	*Numbness.* This is the absence of feelings. This is our defense mechanism, used by our mind, to cope with such a shocking revelation. A person may even feel like they are dreaming at this time and nothing seems real. They just shut down because they are so overwhelmed. This can confuse the child because they had intense feelings for Nana and now they feel nothing. They can't even cry at this time. This can last for a few days to several weeks.

"I was enveloped in numbness, and absence of feeling so deep the bottom was lost from view." So says Haruki Murakami.

Prairiecrow in a web posting says: *"I mostly feel numb, and my question is this: Is this normal, or one way that grief can go? I've only cried once since she died, and the rest of the time I just feel tired, distracted, and vaguely pointless. No painful sorrow. No longing for her presence. Just a calm that also makes me uneasy, because I'm afraid of what's going to happen when it breaks."*

G.	*Lonely.* What kind of regular influence did Nana have on your child? The closer they were to her the more loneliness they will experience. They miss the interaction from her. She may have held an important place in their heart. Grandma made them feel significant, wanted and special. She may have been the one to make them smile, or who took them special places. Now there is a great big empty hole in their life. Nana may have been the one with whom they felt most comfortable to talk and share ideas or get advice. Make sure you get them to talk about the fun things they did with her. Ask them how they remember Nana.

H.	*Guilt.* Maybe there are unresolved issues or the last thing they said was really nasty and now they are living with that guilt. A child can feel like they are actually the cause of the death. Recalling the bad incident can start them thinking that if they had done something different that the death would not have happened. They may go through a lot of "What ifs…" If only I had done better in school, helped more around the house, not fought with my brother/sister so much.

I.   *Worried.* Children don't have as much control of their lives as do adults. They are dependent. so they don't know what is going to happen when a parent dies. They may be worried about their place in this "new" family. They may wonder how they are going to survive or how their life is going to change. Some children actually look after their parents who can't handle the burden. They can become very worried about the future.

J.   *Fear.* It is when a person we know so closely dies, that we are also reminded that we too are mortal, and one day we will die. Our image of invulnerability is either cracked or crushed. This is when people think about their own life after they die and what is going to happen to them. Will they, themselves, be accepted by God when they die? Their fear and concern may also cause them to ask where their loved one has gone and if they were ready to meet God. They can also have fear about how you will face life without them if they were to die.

K.   *Sleeping.* I put it in this category because sometimes people use sleep to escape the emotional struggles of life. If you aren't awake, you don't have to think about their death, and how you are going to handle the loss. Another reason the person may need to sleep is because emotional drain makes us tired. One of the ways my youngest daughter would face the stresses of life, as a child, was to go into a closet, curl up, and go to sleep. When she woke up she was better able to face life again. Are they sleeping too much? Is their amount of sleep indicating that they are doing so to avoid facing life? Be discerning about their sleep habits when they are in grief.

L.   *Emancipation.* Some children have been so hurt by the person who died that they actually feel relief when the person dies. Perhaps they were physically, emotionally, sexually or verbally abused for many years, and now that source of hurt is gone. They may feel conflicted and have guilt about their feelings, because now they are free from the hurt, but feel they should be sad because the person died. Being free from the abuser can be elating.

As you can see there are a wide range of possible emotions that can be expressed in your child when they face a loss or difficulty in life. There is an old saying, "To be forewarned is to be forearmed." Advanced warning gives us an advantage so we are not caught off guard to possible difficulties.

CHAPTER FIVE: AFTER NANA DIES

Kelly's Story:

Kelly makes some powerful comments from her personal experience of how she was hurt by the way her parents failed to share with her during the dying and death process of her grandfather. Again, I make comments in parentheses.

> *Things I would change in the way my parents handled the death of my first grandfather when I was 9. They didn't speak of him or his death. For whatever reason they did not show us their hurt or pain that they must have also carried. They did not speak about him with us children that I recall after we buried him. We never went to the cemetery that I recall. They treated his memory like it was okay that he is gone. Perhaps they didn't talk about him because it might hurt. They treated it like his life was a secret. I wish they would have kept him alive in memories because I only have a few memories of the man I grew up behind. I should have a million memories but I don't. I have blocked him out I guess.*

> *As an adult when I lost my hubby we had two grandsons. Their dad had a hard time with the loss of his dad and brother. The result was that he only went to the funeral home one day and that was for two hours. He didn't even bring his sons, so they were never allowed to say good bye to their Grandpa. Later when they came to visit they didn't understand why Grandpa Tom and Uncle Grant weren't with me.*

> *I think parents truly believe kids can't handle the issues of death because of their own inadequacies of how to talk to their kids or grandkids about dying or death. Instead of being open about it*

when there is a sudden death, or it has been coming for some time, they just ignore the children's need in this area.

I think the more kids are in tune, by being told what is happening and explained things, the better it is. Kids aren't so afraid of death. They should be able to cry. I never felt I was allowed to talk or cry about my losses to this day.

I don't feel I have grieved yet nor been able to express my losses, or talk about my losses because of the fear I might upset someone or it might hurt someone. I think kids should be able to talk or cry or even laugh if they want.

(Kelly makes a very important point. The way you deal with your children during this difficult time can have long term effects on their life. It will color how they face difficult times for years to come and perhaps for a life time.)

Another note if the grandparent is sick. Take a child to a family member's funeral that isn't close to them so it's not such a shock to them what they see someone they know. Let them ask questions and touch the person if they want to ... then it's not so much of a shock seeing grandma or grandpa sleeping and not getting up to play with them or talk to them. I swear my grandpa moved. He didn't, but as a young kid I knew he was supposed to be moving.

After the death:

What are some things to keep in mind for your child the days after grandma's death? Provide an atmosphere in which your child can talk and ask questions. They need to talk about their feelings. "Do you feel sad? Alone? Angry? Would you like to talk about it? I love you and want to help you." "If you don't want to talk now we can talk later." Don't press them, but ask a question and let them think on it and answer when they are ready.

Immediately after a death things can get confusing. Lots of people drop over and the kids can get lost in the shuffle. Make sure the children are eating properly. Allow them to get out and get some exercise and make sure that they get enough sleep. Just as a car needs to be refueled to continue to get you around, so we all need fuel that sleep, food and exercise give us to function properly. Exercise is very important, for that is a means of letting off 'steam' or pent up energy that comes from grief and sorrow.

Non-verbal support is important. Sometimes we are hurting so much that we don't want to say anything. Sitting or walking and being quiet can be what some children need. Sometimes just holding them on your lap, or sitting next to them on a couch or lying on the bed together while you hold them can help them a lot. Let them know that they don't have to say anything unless they want to. Hurt can cause some to just go silent while they process or grieve.

Allow your children to teach you. Ask them what they understand about death and what it means. Let them tell you what the death means to them, and then listen quietly. Don't correct their misconceptions right away. Allow them to express things. You can't help them if you don't know what they are thinking, so be a good listener before you start to teach them. You can teach them by sharing what you believe and why.

Recognize that each child is at a different stage mentally and emotionally in the way they grasp death. Be sensitive to that reality. A younger child may have a better concept of death than an older child. Your questions will help you discern what they understand or don't yet comprehend. As you have made your journey through life you find this truth as factual with adults as with children.

Getting back to routine is very important for children. Get them back to school in a timely manner. Let them spend time with their friends. Give them some computer or TV time by themselves. We downplay kids time on the computer. It is often a way in which they get a release from their frustrations.

I had parents come to me one time because their child had mentioned suicide. They asked me to talk with him. As we talked, he shared how he came home after school and played his computer games. He got in trouble and he was grounded from playing his games. He then went on to say that he had no release after school from all that was going on and he didn't know what to do with himself. That is why he got so frustrated. He got back on the computer and there was never another word about suicide. Not all cases are that simple but it was true for this nine year old boy. After the funeral make sure your children get back to some kind of normal routine as soon as possible.

Your child needs their friends during and after the death of Nana. Allow them to spend time with their friends. You may even want to talk to their friend and let them know what happened and you may even go so far as to talk to your child's friend about how to treat your child during this time and even how long it can go on. Encourage them to get your child to talk about Nana and tell favorite stories about her. Friends may be able to relate to your child in a way that you can't, so helping their friend know what they can do to help the grieving process for your child can be of benefit to you as well as your child.

Make sure you avoid alcohol during this time. Alcohol or drugs can prevent you from experiencing the grief that you need to experience in working through your loss. Such avoidance can actually make you more depressed. It will prevent you from properly engaging with others and your children. There was a man in my church whose mother died and he was so distraught that he was drinking before, during and after each of the visitation sessions and before the memorial service itself. I talked with him afterwards and he said that this caused him to not remember most of what happened during those days.

Just as you need to allow your children the freedom to cry, feel numb and be angry, you need to be able to do that yourself. In your mind you tell yourself that you have to be strong and you deny yourself the freedom to express your emotions. It's not a bad thing for your children to see you cry, and maybe even cry with you. You are showing them that Nana was important to you as well.

Sometimes the person who has died creates such a vast void in your child's life that they close down and won't let you get in. This may be the time to see a professional counselor or trained pastor who can help your child move on with their life.

CHAPTER SIX: VISITING THE FUNERAL HOME

Josh's story:

Josh shares his concerns with telling his children about the death of grandpa. Even though the children were only two and three at the time they expressed concerns that perhaps you share.

In these exerts you will recognize that even though they didn't know exactly what to say, they still realized they had to inform their children and tell them the truth. My comments are in parentheses.

1. *I believe that the only information that would have helped us while telling our children was how we would react to the information.*(Dealing with our own grief during this time may be harder on us than on our children.)
2. *We knew how much the kids loved Grandpa and knew that they would miss him. We still had to tell them ahead of time. We couldn't just wait until it happened.*
3. *My wife and I are raising our kids to tell the truth. We did not, and would not hold back anything from our children. We told them that Great Grandpa was sick with cancer and the doctors could not help him, and he would be going to Heaven soon. Just be truthful to your kids. In the end it is the best solution.*
4. *The most frustrating part was handling our grieving process around them. We tried not to show our emotions around them, but that is sometimes not possible. We just explained to them that we miss Great Grandpa and talk about the good times we had with him.*

The Funeral:

Should you take your child to the funeral home? Over my 39 years as pastor I have heard the parent's reasons of why they don't want to take their children to the funeral home, and many parents feel very comfortable taking their children to the funeral home. You have to make the decision for yourself and your family. You know their personality and needs. One thing to keep in mind is that if a child really wants to go to the funeral home, take their request seriously. For many it is very important for them to see Nana for the last time.

My daughter and husband did not bring their children to see my wife when she was close to death, but they did bring them to the funeral home. They were five and nine. I think it is good to take children to the funeral home to see grandma or grandpa or other loved ones. Death is a reality of life that they need to experience. Just as a funeral helps adults accept the reality of a person's death, so it helps your child in the same way. It can be very difficult on them but it is very needful. It also offers relatives and friends a time to talk to them about Nana and tell their stories about her.

If this is the first time taking your child to a funeral home, think of it as their training time. You are going to teach them how to act and respond in their grief. It is wise to sit them down and talk with them. Prior to the funeral it will be a very busy time, but your children are still going to be with you afterwards and they need to learn how to personally deal with death. If they are left to their own imagination they can come up with untrue and unrealistic ideas that they may carry with them through their life.

Talking Points

Here are some talking points that may be helpful to address with them before going to the funeral home. This list is not exhaustive but a good guide line to help you touch on important concerns. Remember, your children are a blank slate and they have no knowledge of what to expect, so this is a very important talk you will have with them.

- Inform them of some of the things they will see.
- Talk about the casket or the cremation urn they will see.

- Describe what grandma will be like in the casket.
- Let them know that they can touch her and that she will be cold because the life has gone out of her.
- Talk about their behavior at the funeral home: it is not a place to run around, play games and be loud.
- Talk about the respect that needs to be shown.
- Talk about how people may act. Some will cry, some will be warm, some will crack jokes, some will need hugs, some will tell stories, some will ask them about Nana and some will not say much at all.
- Tell them it is good to talk with people about Nana. Encourage them to ask adults who knew Nana what they remember about her.
- Encourage them to go around and look at the pictures of Nana and watch the video about her.
- When you get there show them where the bathroom is.
- Many funeral homes have an area where you can bring in food and the kids should know where that is.
- Some funeral homes have a play area for the children so familiarize them this area after you get there.
- Ask them if they have any questions.
- Tell them they can come to you at any time if they have questions.

What are some talking points that would be helpful to address before going to the memorial service?

- Let them know that you will be arriving early and greeting the guests.
- Do they know how to greet adults? When shaking hands look people in the eye, greet them and answer questions.
- Let them know where they will sit.
- Inform them that there will be a speaker who will talk about Nana and then share words of encouragement.
- Usually, after the service, not everyone gets up at once but they are dismissed row by row to go by the casket, to say their final good bye. The family is the last to go to say good bye. You will have specific customs in your area of the country you should share.
- Go up to the casket and tell Nana good bye and if you want you can give her a kiss.

- People go to the car and follow the Hurst to the cemetery.
- Pastor has a few more things to say at the grave side. Maybe there will be military honors.
- It is the tradition in some places to watch the casket as it is lowered into the ground.
- If there are flowers on the casket, then each family member is free to take one as a remembrance.
- Let them know if there is going to be a dinner afterwards.

I have one final word on the topic of talking with your children. It would be good to talk about some of these things before someone you know dies. As Kelly mentioned earlier, take them to the funeral of a person they don't know so well so they can observe. Explain what they are doing as the service progresses. If you can't go to a service, just talk about what happens at a funeral home when someone dies.

This is not complicated, but it can relieve a lot of their tensions and concerns.

CHAPTER SEVEN: ALLOW GRIEF TO DO ITS WORK

As a pastor I see the spiritual side of death and how to face death. I have noticed that even those who have not taken God seriously through life, often take the time to investigate how God fits into the big picture of their life when tragedy strikes. They may even consider more seriously how God may fit into their own life. When we are hurting it is not unusual to turn to other resources for help and understanding.

God is a very important part of the equation, not just in death but also in life. Death causes us to evaluate life and how God fits in, even for those already in the faith. Understanding a biblical reason for death helps one in dealing with the death of others in their own mind. How can we help our children in a meaningful way if we haven't dealt with the issues of death, dying and God ourselves? Understanding how to grieve and deal with our own issues of pain helps us, in turn, to know how to guide our children through their grieving process. It is when we understand a greater purpose in the death of a loved one, that we grow stronger and move on with purpose in life.

When you think of the God of the Bible helping us in our grief you recognize that He is well equipped to help us in this time of sorrow. He is all-knowing so he knows how we hurt and what our specific needs are. He is love so he knows our heart and how to care for us in our time of need. He is the God of all comfort who knows how to comfort us in our suffering. He is the healer of broken hearts. He is also a God who knows how facing this death can prepare us for some unknown purpose in our future.

In Dr. Bob Kellemen's book, God's *Healing for Life's Losses,* he addresses suffering from a biblical perspective and the stages through which we can grow. The responses on the left of the chart below are common knowledge, but the responses on the right show the way one can grow in their faith through their suffering. Even though this review doesn't go into detail of how one goes through each of these stages it presents you with the main points that help you see that working through your grief is a process and takes work on your part. It reveals the higher purpose that God has in mind as you work through your grief. It also reminds you that your pain and grief doesn't go away just because you have faith in God. I think you will appreciate Bob's practical insights into this process of grief. I recommend his book for further help in understanding each point more fully.

Biblical Sufferology Chart

Sustaining in Suffering: Stages of Hurt–"It's Normal to Hurt and Necessary to Grieve"		
Stage	**Typical Grief Response**	**Biblical Grief Response**
1	Denial/Isolation	Candor: Honesty with Myself
2	Anger/Resentment	Complaint: Honesty with God
3	Bargaining/Works	Cry: Asking God for Help
4	Depression/Alienation	Comfort: Receiving God's Help
Healing in Suffering: Stages of Hope "It's Possible to Hope and Supernatural to Grow"		
Stage	**Typical Acceptance Response**	**Biblical Growth Response**
5	Regrouping	Waiting: Trusting with Faith
6	Deadening	Wailing: Groaning with Hope
7	Despairing/Doubting	Weaving: Perceiving with Grace
8	Digging Cisterns	Worshipping: Engaging with Love

"The first four stages involve sustaining in suffering. The second four stages relate to healing in suffering.

Please, always remember that these "stages" are a relational process, not sequential steps. Grieving and growing is not a neat, predictable package. It isn't a tidy procedure.

Grieving and growing is messy because life is messy. Moving through hurt to hope is a two-steps-forward, one-step-backwards endeavor. We don't "conquer a stage" and never return to it.

Rather than picturing a linear, step-by-step route, imagine a three dimensional maze with many possible paths, frequent detours, backtracking, and even the ability to reside in more than one "stage" at the same time.

However, positive movement is possible. In fact, it is promised. You can find God's healing for your losses. You can find hope in your hurt.

Whatever your grieving experience has been like up to this point, don't quit. Don't give up.

Grief is a journey. Experiencing the biblical reality of the journey of grief recognizes that it's normal to hurt and necessary to grieve. Learn how to move from denial to personal honesty (candor), from anger to honesty with God (complaint), from bargaining to asking God for help (crying out), and from depression to receiving God's help (comfort).

Stay on the path. Experience the biblical reality that it's possible to hope and supernatural to grow. Learn how to move from regrouping to trusting with faith (waiting on God), from deadening to groaning with hope (wailing to God), from despair to perceiving with grace (weaving in God's truth), and from digging cisterns to engaging with love (worshipping God and ministering to others).

God truly does provide you with everything you need for life and godliness. Through the Word of God, the Spirit of God, and the people of God, you have all you need for your healing journey."[4]

Dr. Kellemen's book *God's Healing for Life's Losses* is published by GriefShare, an organization with which I am familiar and really appreciate. I have taught the GriefShare course in the churches I have been involved in over the years. It is taught across the country. It is a thirteen week class taught in churches and in the community. You can go to http://www.griefshare.org to get more information about the book or a class near you. This is a video based class and covers so many areas of concern that you face in your grieving process. As I conduct the courses one thing I appreciate hearing from the people and usually in a surprised expression is "*I thought I was the only one that experienced that.*" I highly recommend this grief group to help you in working through your grief and loss.

Here is how GriefShare describes themselves on their webpage. *"What is GriefShare? GriefShare is a friendly, caring group of people who will walk alongside you through one of life's most difficult experiences. You don't have to go through the grieving process alone.*

GriefShare seminars and support groups are led by people who understand what you are going through and want to help. You'll gain access to valuable GriefShare resources to help you recover from your loss and look forward to rebuilding your life.

The grieving process

I will not go into a lot of detail about the grieving process in this book, for there are many excellent books available that addressed this topic in a fine manner. Let me share an overview of the grieving process.

The grieving process is not an event but a process over time. The grieving process, for most, will not be over in four to twelve weeks. The child may not talk about Nana after the first few weeks but the grieving process is going on inside of them. It is typical that the grieving process can take one to two years. Sometimes it can take a year before some children start manifesting some of their grief. Make sure you monitor your child in regular conversation about their grief. Talk with them. Don't pressure them. They may seem all right in their actions, but you don't know the struggles going on in their mind. Intentionally maintain a good relationship with your child. You do that by getting them to talk and valuing what they have to say and taking them seriously. Listening is so important in relationship and the grieving process. Just as you don't appreciate it when people don't take your seriously, neither does your child like it when you don't take them seriously.

Don't minimize a person's pain by telling them that they need to get over it, or get on with their life. Recognizing that the grieving process may take quite a while, doesn't mean that their grief will always be intense all the time. Grief is like the waves of the lake that come along unexpectedly and regularly as we work through our memories. This is especially true during that first year as you and your child go through anniversaries, birthdays and holidays. These cause us to reflect and miss Nana because she will not be there to be part of our celebration and interaction. Her influence is now gone from your gatherings.

Take time to remember Nana at each holiday. Talk about memories, what you miss most about her not being there. Recall funny or meaningful stories. Don't be afraid of their tears. Just hold your child and let them cry and be understanding. Don't force them, but allow their sharing to be natural.

I am writing this section as a revision a year after publishing the book. Last week was my wife's birthday and we decided to celebrate it because we were all together visiting my daughter in Colorado. Nancy has been dead for about three and a half years. My daughters are both in their forties. We sat around the table and talked of our memories of Nana. We laughed and cried. We talked of how her life touched and changed our lives. What a great time it was. It was not forced but a time of sharing what was on our heart. We all needed this time and it was not only refreshing but healing.

Make sure you provide opportunities like this for your family on occasion. These are the kinds of times that help our hearts to mend. The healing process is a time to focus on establishing closer relationships. Sharing memories and how the person has touched our life, builds the kinds of bonds that help us to heal and go on in life with greater strength and resolve. Look for creative ways to bring up memories of Nana for at least two to three years and at special occasions like weddings and family reunions

As I was thinking about a concluding thought to this section on grief I was reminded how death disrupts our circle of community. The grieving process is a redevelopment of that social community in which we look for others to help fill in the gap that death created. We also need to become the one who develops community with others to help them in their journey. Our goal should not be just to look for others to help us, but we need to eventually look for ways to be involved with others so we can help them. The following came as a result of that thinking process of how community and relationships helps us throughout period of grief.

What is the essence of the grieving process?

Death is the separation of a loved one or friend from *our social community*. Just as each denomination of paper currency has a different value, so each loss has a different value in our life. Some represent greater losses than others. Each person related to our life in a different manner. With some we were more dependent on because of the needs they helped fulfill in our being together. Every time we do something the other person usually did we again feel the pain of their loss. So each death leaves a different sized hole in our soul.

Grieving is the process of building up the strength and closeness of *our social community* that has now become smaller because of death. It is filling in the gap, that has been created by their death, with love, involvement, and concern from others. It is learning that our life has a purpose, even though that person is no longer there to walk with us in our journey. We must not give up living and be determine to go on with a productive life, and influence others in a positive way.

Hope is the recognition that *our social community* will be reestablished in the future, not just with that person again, but with God, and a greater community of people whom we will learn to love as they become an integral part of our eternal existence.

James Olah
6/18/2014

FINALE: WRAPPING IT UP

Nothing said in this book is profound. It is just simple advice arranged in a manner to help you guide your child through a difficult time in their life. The more we know, the easier it is to know what to do. To be informed equips you to be a better guide for your child.

When my children started driving I would talk to them about certain driving scenarios and what to do. I told them that if an animal runs out in front of them it is safer to hit the animal rather than run off the road, or swerve in front of another car. That way they can avoid destruction of the vehicle, injury or death. Some months later they were with mom in the car and an animal ran in front of them while on a busy expressway. The dog was hit, but there was no accident. The dog did get up and run off. The point I am making is that because they thought about what they would do before it happened, they didn't have to think twice about how to handle the situation in a proper way. It could have saved their life.

In the same way, it is important to know ahead of time how you are going to handle the situation when Nana is found to be seriously ill or has died. I trust that this book has given you the kind of information that will help you to better know how to prepare your child to face their difficult time or to guide them through loss and grief.

May this book be an encouragement to you in dealing with, what can be, one of life's more complicated situations.

ABOUT THE AUTHOR

 Rev. James Olah was born in Muskegon, Michigan. He received his pastoral training at the Grand Rapids School of the Bible and Music. He also attended a couple of community colleges and William Tyndale College of Detroit, Michigan. He served as a youth pastor for nine years and pastored two churches during the next thirty four years.

In Grand Rapids, at the same school, he met his wife to who he was married for 43 years. Nancy served faithfully with him during those years. She died in 2012 after a short bout with cancer.

During his years of pastoring he gained a great deal of experience from calling on sick and dying people in their homes as well as in the hospital. Toward the end of his ministry he became a hospice chaplain for three years. He also taught several Grief Share classes. He has a heart for the hurting and dying.

In recent years he has authored ten books. He writes on a variety of topics. One series deals with marital relationships and another series focuses on issues of the Christian faith. This book is part of a series on facing the difficulties in life. He also published two children's books.

OTHER BOOKS BY JAMES OLAH

Death and Suffering: A Christian Perspective
Biblical considerations for working through the "Why" questions and the purpose of your tragedies
Seeing God and His ways in the difficulties of life
Dealing with Tragedy as a Christian
Book 1 of Facing the Difficulties of Life Series
Kindle: http://www.amazon.com/dp/B006SJKSPO

What is the Tone of Your Communication?
How does tone of voice affect your communication?
Book 3 of Improving Your Relationship Series
Kindle: http://www.amazon.com/dp/B004Y020KU
Paper: http://www.amazon.com/dp/1492226319

The Dynamics of Communication and Sex
Effective Keys to Preventing Relationship Breakdowns
Enjoying the Benefits of Maintaining a Healthy Sex Life in your Marriage
Book 2 of Improving Your Relationship Series
Kindle: http://www.amazon.com/dp/B0072BVUJU
Paper: http://www.amazon.com/dp/1494238349

Getting to Know You
Questions to help prepare for marriage
300 + questions to ask in developing a relationship
Plus other helpful articles
Book 1 of Improving Your Relationship Series
Kindle: http://www.amazon.com/dp/B003VTZW7I

Helps for Young Christians
For Believers Who Seek Guidance and Direction in their Walk of Faith.
Book 2 of Christian Faith Series
Kindle: http://www.amazon.com/dp/B008FU0OY4
Paper: http://www.amazon.com/dp/1494399601/

Helps for Christians
Securing loose ends of your faith
Issues in which many get stuck or come to faulty conclusion
Book 3 of Christianity Faith Series
Kindle: http://www.amazon.com/dp/B00NVQR6C0
Paper: http://www.amazon.com/dp/1502533782

Town of Salvation
How does Christianity differ from the Religions of the World?
What does the Bible Teach about Salvation?
Book 1 of "Christianity Faith Series
Kindle: http://www.amazon.com/dp/B007ZJYA5A

How Fast? How Far? How Big?
Fun Facts for Kids about Speed, Distance and Size in Our
Solar System and Universe. Trivia to Amaze Your Friends
1 - Children's Fun Learning Series
Kindle: http://www.amazon.com/dp/B00GI0SMLA

Sploring with Papa
A fun Story of a Grandson and Grandpa Exploring (sploring) Rail Road
Tracks and an Old Barn, as told by Trinity
2 - Children's Fun Learning Series
Kindle: http://www.amazon.com/dp/B00HBZ1ZW4

Check out the Author Page:
http://www.amazon.com/James-Olah/e/B005WLXP5O

Pastor Olah is available for speaking engagements about the book.

If you liked this book please write a review on Amazon.

[1] Children and Grief: What They Know, How They Feel, How to Help by Robin F. Goodman, Ph.D. http://www.aboutourkids.org/articles/children_grief_what_they_know_how_they_feel_how_help Used by permission.

[2] Holy Bible: Hebrews 9:27

[3] Lisa Athan, Executive Director of Grief Speaks (griefspeaks.com) Used by permission.

[4] Materials comes from Dr. Robert Kellemen's article "A Biblical Model of Grieving": http://www.rpmministries.org/2010/07/a-biblical-model-of-grieving/ This article comes from Dr. Kellemen's book, *God's Healing for Life's Losses*. To learn more about *God's Healing for Life's Losses* you can visit here: http://www.rpmministries.org/writing/gods-healing-for-lifes-losses/ Used by Permission